Street Art Festivals

by Abbie Rushton

OXFORD
UNIVERSITY PRESS

This is a street art festival. Artists paint on the streets.

How can I see street art?

Street art festivals are held in lots of towns.

This is the Darwin Street Art Festival.

This is the Boon Street Art Festival.

Some artists put on a show. Look at the artists perform.

stilt

What is street art painted on?

It is painted on towers.

tower

This street art is on a bus shelter.
Look at the bright splashes of paint!

How do street artists paint?

They check with the owner.

The artist might splash paint on the bricks.

This scrap of fabric mops up drips.

This art is up high. The artist needs a ladder and a harness.

How can I join in?

Grab a map and some strong boots.
Join the festival crowds.

You can pedal, too. Remember to strap on a helmet!

Go and meet the street artists. They like to chat.

You can get tips from artists. They can show you how to paint street art.

Go and see a street art festival near you. You will love it!

Look Back

Encourage students to use the images to review the topic.